Drugs and Crime

Jeffrey Shulman

Illustrated by Larry Raymond

TWENTY-FIRST CENTURY BOOKS
FREDERICK, MARYLAND

Published by
Twenty-First Century Books
38 South Market Street
Frederick, Maryland 21701

Text Copyright © 1991
Twenty-First Century Books

Illustrations Copyright © 1991
Larry Raymond

Printed in the United States of America

10 9 8 7 6 5 4 3 2 1

Editorial and Research Assistant:
Teresa Rogers

Library of Congress Cataloging in Publication Data

Shulman, Jeffrey
Drugs and Crime
Illustrated by Larry Raymond

(A Social Impact Book)
Includes glossary and index.
Summary: Examines the connection between illegal drugs and crime
and what is being done to break that "straight-line relationship."
1. Narcotics and crime—United States—Juvenile literature.
2. Drug abuse—United States—Juvenile literature.
3. Drug traffic—United States—Juvenile literature.
4. Narcotics, Control of—United States—Juvenile literature.
[1. Narcotics and crime. 2. Drug abuse. 3. Narcotics, Control of.]
I. Raymond, Larry, ill. II. Title.
III. Series: The Social Impact Series.
HV5825.35   1991
363.4'5'0973—dc20   90-24369 CIP AC
ISBN 0-941477-60-6

Contents

1

The Straight Line

"The drug problem affects every American. It affects each of us in various ways.

"There is a straight-line relationship between the violent crime in our communities and the abuse of drugs.

"There is a straight-line relationship between every coke sniffer and every crack smoker in this country and the murder that takes place within all our communities."

Richard Thornburgh
U.S. Attorney General

Richard Thornburgh is the Attorney General of the United States. He is the country's top law enforcement official. His job is to lead the nation in the fight against crime. As you can imagine, it's a big job.

And Richard Thornburgh has a big problem.

The problem is drugs and crime. The problem is that there is a "straight-line relationship" between drug use and crime. Nearly 2,000 people are arrested every day for drug-related crimes. In many major cities, almost one-half of the people arrested for serious crimes test positive for drug use. The United States spends billions of dollars each year on criminal investigations related to drugs. And the cost of keeping drug dealers in prison adds millions more.

Numbers like these, however, don't show the full impact of drug-related crime on us and our society. They don't show the overcrowded courts and prisons. They don't show the violence in our schools and on our streets. They don't show how drugs threaten the safety of our offices and workplaces. They don't show the hospital emergency rooms overflowing with the victims of drug use and drug-related violence. They don't show how our national parks and state forests are becoming a secret home for drug operations.

Most of all, the numbers don't show the many thousands of lives lost every year to drug use and drug-related crime.

The problem of drugs and crime is much more than numbers. The problem is people. Of course, part of the problem is people who simply don't care about the costs of drug-related crime, people who want to make a "fast buck" by dealing drugs. But that's only part of the problem.

The problem is also people who don't understand the "straight-line relationship" between drug use and crime. They say, "I know it's against the law, but I'm not hurting anyone." They say that they're just smoking a little grass on the weekend. They say they're just trying some cocaine at a party. They say they're not giving drugs to young people or fighting in the streets with rival gangs.

"So what's the problem?" they ask.

- The problem is that drug use is against the law.

People who use drugs are breaking the law. A law is like an agreement that the people in a country make together. They make laws to protect individuals and the society as a whole from dangerous products and dangerous kinds of behavior. But when people use drugs, they break that agreement and weaken the very idea of the law. When people use drugs, they're using dangerous substances that not only hurt them, but are certain to hurt other people as well.

You know about pollution. You probably know how pollution hurts everyone. You know that when a factory dumps poisonous waste into our air or water, it hurts the people who drink the water and breathe the air. Pollution isn't just a problem for the people who make it. It's a problem for all of us. And that's why we have laws to protect our society and to keep our world clean and safe.

Drugs are a kind of pollution. They poison the people who use them. And the poison of drugs hurts everyone in our society.

- The problem is that drug use leads people to break the law.

Drug use changes the way the brain works. Using drugs changes the way people think, feel, and behave. It causes people to behave in ways that are strange, dangerous, or violent. It can cause people to behave in ways that get them in trouble with the law.

The repeated use of drugs can lead to addiction, the constant need or craving for a drug. The repeated use of drugs can change the way the brain works so much that addicts need drugs to feel normal. They feel that they must have drugs. They feel sick without drugs. That's why drug addicts so frequently commit crimes: to get money to buy more drugs.

- The problem is that drug use is part of a network of criminal activity.

It's a network of drug producers and pushers that runs throughout the nation, from the street corners of rural Georgia to the mountains of western Wyoming, from California's national forests to the skyscrapers of New York City. As the Attorney General says, "No community is exempt from the ravages of the drug trade. Drug-trafficking enterprises have infiltrated all of our country, from our biggest cities to the smallest villages and towns in our heartland."

- The problem is that any drug use supports this network of criminal activity.

Smoking marijuana every now and then or trying cocaine once in a while keeps the drug producers and pushers in business. It keeps them in the business of making and selling drugs. And part of that business *is* giving drugs to young people. It's good for business. And part of that business *is* fighting to defend a gang's drug territory. It's just part of doing business.

This is a book about drugs and crime.

It's about the "drug kingpins" of South America, who preside over vast cocaine empires.

It's about the California marijuana growers, who use our national forests to hide thousands of acres of marijuana plants.

It's about the political leaders and even some law enforcement officials who betray the public trust by using drugs or allowing drugs to be used.

It's about the crime "families" and criminal gangs that control the drug network.

It's about the street-corner crack dealer and the street-corner addict.

And it's about the people who use drugs just for a good time, the so-called "casual" users who keep the worldwide drug network working.

One part of this book is about alcohol. Although alcohol is legal for adults to use, it is a major factor in many crimes committed by people both young and old. And drunk driving is the most frequently committed crime in the United States today.

This is also a book about the fight against drug-related crime. It's a book about the thousands of men and women trying to break the "straight-line relationship" between drugs and crime. And that job means much more than catching drug smugglers or busting crack houses.

As the Attorney General knows, it means getting people to see how the poison of drugs hurts everyone:

"The real drug war will not be won in the cocaine jungles of South America where terrorists prowl or on the inner-city street corners where the street gangs shoot it out. The real war must be fought on the battlefield of values.

"The drug war will not be won by drug agents or by prosecutors in the courtroom. Although law enforcement is part of the solution, we will only achieve victory when a winning battle is fought in the classroom, in the workplace, in the community, and, most important, in the family. The nation must reclaim more than its streets from the drug dealers; we must reclaim a value system that emphasizes, once again, the virtues of self-respect, self-reliance, and the integrity of our mind and spirit."

It's not going to be an easy job. But it can be done. And you can help by learning about the "straight-line relationship" between drugs and crime. You can help by understanding that your actions are part of a network of actions that affect everyone. You can help by taking a stand against drugs and against crime—and by taking a stand for yourself and your family, for your friends, and for all the people who share your neighborhood, your city, and your nation.

2

The Drug Network

It was a typical month. The newspapers told the same story they have told time and time again.

They told the story of drugs and crime.

A three-year-old girl in New York City was critically wounded by a stray bullet fired in a drug dispute. She was the seventh child shot that month in a shocking wave of violence, much of it related to the disputes of rival drug gangs. David Dinkins, the mayor of New York City, announced plans to hire more than 1,000 additional police officers.

The mayor of Washington, D.C., was convicted on one count of cocaine possession.

The former county attorney for King George County, Virginia, pleaded guilty to distributing marijuana and cocaine.

Sheriffs of four counties in Kentucky were charged with taking payoffs to protect drug dealers.

Police in Frederick, Maryland, arrested a 12-year-old boy for selling crack cocaine. "This was not the first time he's been dealing," said Captain Pierce Stine of the city police.

South American drug gangs are beginning to build "a vast cocaine empire in Western European countries," according to a report by international police groups. The new markets in Spain, Holland, and Italy "have now replaced the United States as the biggest market for cocaine," a Bogota, Colombia, newspaper reported.

These are just some of the actual pictures of drugs and crime. Every day, there are hundreds of others. In fact, there are so many different pictures of drugs and crime that it may be difficult for people to see how each one forms a part of the overall network of drug-related crime. It may be difficult to see how all the pieces of the drug puzzle fit together.

It's hard to say where the network of drugs and crime begins. Does it begin with the farmer who grows the coca plant that is the source of cocaine? Does it begin with the drug dealer who sells coke to make money? Or does it begin with the person who wants to buy cocaine to get high?

Perhaps one way to understand this network is to think of the drug trade as a business. The purpose of the drug business, like that of any other business, is to make money. A business tries to make money by developing a product or service that people want. In other words, a business supplies a product or service that is in demand. There must be a steady demand for the product or service that a business supplies. Otherwise, that business won't be in business for long.

Imagine that you want to start a business. Let's say that you decide to go into the business of selling gasoline. You know that there's a big demand today for this product. "Just look at all the cars, buses, and planes," you say. "Look how many gasoline stations there are. And don't forget the motorcycles and the lawn mowers and the powerboats. Hey, I'm going to be a millionaire!"

Well, maybe you will. But first you'd better take a look at the whole picture. Your business is part of a much larger network of business activities.

"So what do I have to do to get started?" you ask.

To get started, you have to get the gasoline. But gasoline is made from the raw material of crude oil. So you have to find a source of this material. There are good sources of crude oil in several places throughout the world. There are many foreign sources, like the oil-producing deserts of the Middle East. And there are also rich sources of crude oil within the United States (we call these domestic sources), like the snow-covered oil fields of Alaska.

So you have to buy the crude oil from the places that produce it. And you have to keep in mind that crude oil is not ready to be used as gasoline. It has to be processed before it can be pumped into a gas tank. So you need a processing plant called a refinery to make the gasoline.

And that's not all. Somehow you need to ship the crude oil from your source of raw material to your refinery. Supplies of crude oil are usually loaded onto huge oil tankers or shipped through long pipelines.

Even that's not all. You still need a way to get the gasoline to the people who want it. You need a way to distribute your gasoline, or what is called a distribution system. You need gasoline storage centers. And you need hundreds of trucks to carry gasoline to the thousands of gasoline stations across the country where people can pull in and say, "Fill 'er up."

"All that just to be a millionaire?"

All that—and a whole lot more. From an oil field halfway around the world to the local gas station— that's the network of operations in the gasoline business. And every time people buy gasoline, they are part of that network of operations. They support that network. They keep that network working.

The drug business is a network of operations, too. The drug business, like other businesses, develops a product that many people want to buy. The product is drugs.

The drug trade has its sources of raw materials.

The raw materials of the drug business are the plants from which the drugs come.

- Cocaine is made from the coca plant, which grows in the mountainous areas of Latin America. The four main sources of the U.S. cocaine supply are the South American countries of Ecuador, Bolivia, Colombia, and Peru. More than 400,000 acres of South American farmland are now used to grow the coca plant.

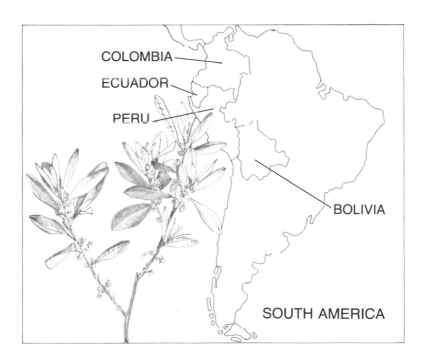

- Heroin is made from the opium poppy. The opium poppy grows best in the warm climate and dry soil of Southeast Asia, in an area known as the Golden Triangle (Burma, Laos, and Thailand); in Southwest Asia, in an area called the Golden Crescent (Pakistan, Iran, and Afghanistan); and in such countries as Mexico, India, and Turkey.

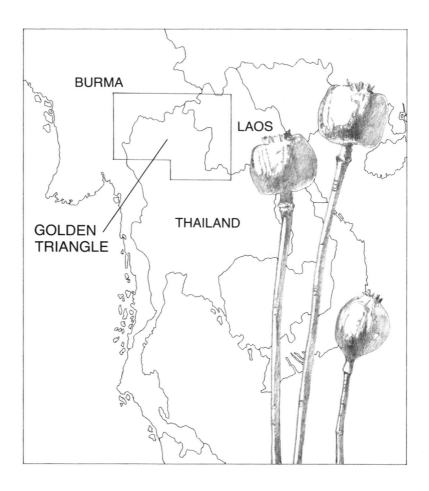

- Marijuana is made from the cannabis, or hemp, plant. Like cocaine and heroin, a good deal of the U.S. supply of marijuana comes from abroad, from countries like Mexico, Jamaica, Thailand, Colombia, and Laos. But, unlike cocaine and heroin, much of the marijuana used in the United States is a domestic crop. Marijuana is grown as part of the drug trade in 46 out of 50 states. It's grown in places like Kentucky's Daniel Boone National Forest and California's Humboldt County. In some rural areas, where other work is hard to find, marijuana growing is the main source of income for many people.

The drug trade has its processing plants, or refineries.

Whether the source of drugs is foreign or domestic, the drug trade depends on the farmers who grow drug-related crops. In many cases, these farmers are very poor, and growing the coca plant or the opium poppy is the only way they can make a living. From hundreds of small farms, the drug harvest has to be taken to a central location to be processed, or refined, and prepared for shipment.

- In remote regions of Latin America, coca growers dry and press the greenish-brown leaves of the coca plant to form a thick coca paste. This paste is processed by treating it with strong chemicals, like sulfuric acid and kerosene, to make the powdery substance known as cocaine.

- The milky-white juice of the poppy seedpods is dried to form a dark, sticky paste. This opium paste is boiled and, like coca paste, is treated with harsh chemicals to make the opiate drugs morphine and heroin.

- The flowering tops and leaves of the cannabis plant are dried and shredded to form the leafy, greenish-brown mixture known as marijuana. Marijuana growers use special growing techniques to increase the strength of their drug crop.

The drug trade has its shipment routes.

The drug harvest has to be carried from the farm to the refinery, and the drug product must be shipped to countries around the world. It is a long journey, and one that must be kept secret. The secret shipment of drugs is called smuggling.

This drug journey may begin on foot or horse-back as drug carriers, often called "mules," transport the drug harvest to the regional refineries. From the refinery, drugs are transported to storage areas where they await shipment overseas. Smugglers use a number of ways to get drugs past the officials whose job is to catch such shipments.

Here are some examples of the different types of smuggling operations:

- From some 2,000 airstrips in the Colombian jungle, drug dealers ship cocaine aboard large transport planes to "drop spots" on the Caribbean islands. From the Caribbean, drug runners race across the water on "cigarette" speedboats to secret destinations in southern Florida or the coastal marshes of Louisiana and Georgia. More than 70 tons of cocaine are shipped to the United States each year.

- Marijuana from Mexico is most often shipped to Texas and California. It is carried over the border crossings hidden aboard cars and trucks. It is carried by "mules" who sneak across the border at night. It is even carried by tourists who are paid by drug dealers to smuggle marijuana shipments. More than 10,000 tons of marijuana are shipped to the United States each year.

- By foot or by horseback, shipments of opium from the Golden Crescent are carried to the busy cities of the Middle East. From here, the shipments are transported on ships to secret laboratories across Europe, where heroin is produced from the opium base. Shipments of heroin are then hidden aboard cargo bound for U.S. cities, especially the port of New York City. More than six tons of heroin are shipped to the United States each year.

The drug trade has its distribution system.

After a shipment of drugs is smuggled into the country, dealers send it to distribution centers, often located in big cities. Here, the drug shipment is stored until it can be sold. From these large storage centers, drug shipments are sold to regional distributors, who provide the drugs to local pushers.

And it's the local pushers who supply cocaine to the 8 million Americans who use it each year; who supply heroin to the more than 500,000 heroin addicts in the United States; and who supply marijuana to the 25 million people who smoke it each year.

Like the gasoline business, the network of the drug business stretches across the globe and reaches to every street corner. And, also like the gasoline business, the network of the drug business is supported by the people who buy its product.

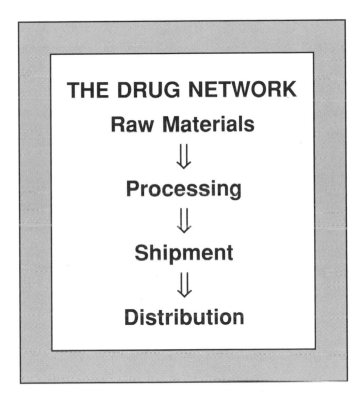

Every time people use drugs, they are part of a network of criminal activity. And every time people use drugs, they help to keep that network of criminal activity working.

The drug business may be like other businesses in some ways. But in two important ways it is unlike any other business.

• The product of the drug business is illegal.

Our society has decided that drugs like cocaine, heroin, and marijuana are so dangerous that it should be against the law to grow, make, buy, or use them. In Chapter 4, you will learn why these drugs are so dangerous. But, for now, it is important to emphasize that just by using illegal drugs people are committing a crime. And they are helping to support a business based on a network of crime—and violence.

• The people in the drug business are criminals.

Drug use puts everyone at risk. The network of the drug trade creates a network of drug-related crime that affects everyone. But some people stand to gain from drug use. They stand to make money from the drug trade.

These people are the drug dealers.

3

The Drug Dealers

Try to picture some friends asking you to smoke a joint at a party or to try cocaine for the first time. Try to picture them saying to you, "Come on. It's not hurting anyone."

What do you say?

It may be hard to imagine that your friends are drug dealers. After all, they're just like you. They're not criminals. They're not murderers. They just want to have a little fun.

But people who ask you to use drugs, whether they are your friends or not, are drug dealers. They are part of the drug network.

Some people think that a drug dealer must be a tough-looking street pusher. They would be surprised to learn that the drug network would not be able to work without the help of bankers, businessmen, lawyers, chemists, accountants, and even law enforcement officials. They would be surprised to learn that a drug dealer is likely to wear a business suit to work or that the network of the drug trade operates like a modern corporation.

There is no one type of drug dealer. There are large, organized groups that run the international drug business. There are secret drug "families" that direct the national distribution system. There are street gangs and motorcycle gangs that fight to control regional drug territories. But, large or small, whether they work in plush offices or on busy street corners, drug dealers rely on threats, bribes, and violence to protect their part of the drug network.

The international flow of drugs is controlled by several large crime groups. Some of the biggest—and most violent—of these crime groups are located in the South American country of Colombia. These groups are known as cartels ("cartel" means a combination of groups who work together to increase business). The Colombian cartels are named after the cities from which they operate. The two largest of these crime groups are the Medellin and Cali cartels.

There is a good reason why these crime groups are located in some of Colombia's major cities. Almost 75 percent of the cocaine and marijuana that is used in the United States comes from the farms of Colombia's drug growers. And this means that the dealers who control the Colombian drug trade have enormous wealth and power.

A recent U.S. Justice Department report says that the influence of the Colombian cartels "has spread to the point where they are a state within a state."

For the poor drug farmers of South America, the drug business means more money than they could hope to make by growing other crops. For the leaders of the drug groups, it means huge mansions, vast drug laboratories, political power, and even private armies. But for the countries of South America, it means a dangerous wave of corruption and violence.

The drug cartels have become, in the words of Colombian President Belisario Betancourt, "empires of blood and violence."

Carlos Lehder, a former leader of the Medellin cartel, puts it this way: "Every so often in this business, someone has to die."

But it is more than every so often. The violence of the drug cartels is an everyday part of business for these groups. Here are just a few pictures of the South American drug business at work:

- Cartel "hit" squads have murdered thousands of Colombian politicians, judges, newspaper editors, police chiefs, and government officials. They have assassinated a Minister of Justice, Supreme Court justices, the Attorney General, and a candidate for the Colombian presidency.

- Pablo Escobar Gaviria, the leader of the Medellin cartel, recently offered a bounty of $500 to $2,000 for each policeman killed in the city of Medellin. Hundreds of police officers have been murdered since then.

- Through bribery and violence, drug dealers have corrupted local and national government officials. Hundreds of Colombian police officers, judges and justice ministry workers, customs agents, and even military leaders are on the payroll of the cartels.

- The drug network has made Medellin "the cocaine and murder capital of the world." During a recent wave of violence, there were 40 drug-related murders a day in the city of Medellin. Today, the murder rate is down to about 12 a day. Most of the dead are between 15 and 24 years old.

- Cartel leaders hire teenage boys to kill rival gang leaders, policemen, and government officials. By one recent count, there are as many as 2,000 of these teenage "hit men."

- Cartel leaders have even bribed the rulers of other countries, including Cuba and Panama, to support the production and shipment of drugs.

- The violence of this drug network is not limited to South American cities. From 1979 to 1982, the city of Miami, Florida, witnessed a wave of violence, including 250 deaths, as rival drug cartels fought to control drug territory. And record murder rates in other cities, such as San Diego and Washington, D.C., have also been linked to drug cartel wars.

The South American drug cartels are not the only large-scale drug groups operating today. A major portion of both the heroin and cocaine trade in the United States is controlled closely by a group of secret crime "families," a criminal network known to law enforcement officials as La Cosa Nostra (LCN). LCN consists of 25 families, each one headed by a boss who runs a criminal network of thousands of members, including underbosses, counselors, street bosses, and "soldiers."

31

Founded in the 1930s, LCN quickly became the most important and violent of the U.S. crime networks.

Today, there are other crime groups challenging the older LCN network for control of the drug trade. Chinese Organized Crime (COC) groups are working with Asian drug-dealing gangs to take over the U.S. heroin market. Jamaican gangs called "posses" deal marijuana and crack cocaine. Motorcycle gangs now control the methamphetamine market. And California street gangs run PCP and crack from coast to coast.

While these groups are smaller than the international drug networks, they are no less violent. According to law enforcement officials, the Jamaican posses alone have killed at least 1,000 people since 1985. The U.S. Justice Department recently provided some vivid pictures of what the drug trade is really about:

> *"The posses have demonstrated a willingness to turn to violence and torture at the slightest provocation. . . . Victims in some homicides were apparently shot in the ankles, knees, and hips before being shot in the head. It also appears that other victims were subjected to scalding hot water before being murdered and dismembered. The posses' violence is directed at anyone who they feel is in their way: members of their group, rival groups, individuals who interfere with their drug territories, wives, girlfriends, and even children."*

"One of the most frightening aspects of the California street gangs is their willingness to direct their violence at each other, at the police, at members of the public—at anyone who stands in the way of their operations. What makes this violence especially frightening is the amount of firepower at their disposal. Where the gangs once had to make do with zip guns, small-caliber rifles, and sawed-off shotguns, they can now acquire semi-automatic rifles and large-caliber handguns."

These are the true pictures of the drug network.

Now, try again to picture some of your friends asking you to smoke a joint at a party or to try cocaine for the first time. Try again to picture them saying to you, "Come on. It's not hurting anyone."

Now, what do you say?

4

Drugs and the Law

The product is illegal drugs. The people who deal drugs are criminals. That's why the drug business is unlike any other business.

It sounds simple enough. But why are there laws against some drugs in the first place? Why aren't they treated like other business products? This is a question that goes to the heart of the problem of drugs and crime. And there is no simple answer.

To begin with, not all drugs are illegal.

- Alcohol is a drug, yet adults are allowed to use alcoholic products.

- Nicotine is a drug, yet adults are allowed to use many different tobacco products, all of which contain nicotine.

- The drug caffeine can be found in many everyday items, like cola soft drinks and chocolate candy bars. Imagine how many police officers we would need if caffeine products were against the law!

So why are other drugs—like cocaine, heroin, and marijuana—against the law?

The main difference has to do with how harmful most people think a drug is. Cocaine, marijuana, heroin, and other drugs are against the law because most people believe that these substances are simply too dangerous for anyone to use. They believe that the dangerous effects these drugs have on the body and the brain are so severe and so immediate that no one should be allowed to try them.

Just because a drug is legal, however, does not necessarily mean that it is safe to use. Everyone agrees that smoking cigarettes is not safe. Everyone knows that cigarette smoke leads to serious health problems. And everyone knows that it is especially dangerous for young people to smoke.

That's why there are many laws to control the use of tobacco products. It is against the law to smoke in many public places. It is also against the law to sell cigarettes to young people. And all tobacco products must carry warnings to alert people to the dangers of using them.

But at this time most people do not believe that the effects of smoking are so dangerous that tobacco products should be outlawed for adults to use. Of course, as time goes by and scientists learn more about the effects of smoking, people may change their minds. They may decide that the effects of smoking tobacco products are too dangerous for anyone to use them. And they may decide to change the laws about products containing nicotine. As we shall see in Chapter 5, the laws about drugs have changed many times, and some drugs that were once legal to use are now against the law.

Everyone knows that alcohol can be dangerous to use. Everyone knows that alcohol can hurt the body. Everyone knows that alcohol can change the way the brain works, causing addiction. And everyone knows that drinking and driving is especially dangerous.

That's why there are many laws to control the use of alcoholic products. There are laws about who can make alcoholic products and where and when they can be sold. It is against the law for young people to use alcohol. Every state has now passed laws against drinking and driving. And in some places alcoholic products are, in fact, against the law for anyone, including adults, to use.

But most people at this time do not believe that the effects of alcohol are so severe and so immediate that alcoholic products should be outlawed for adults to use. This has not always been the case. We will see in Chapter 6 that the laws about using alcohol have also changed and that at one time alcoholic products were against the law for everyone everywhere in the United States.

One reason why we have laws about drugs is that the people who use dangerous drugs put themselves at risk. They risk their health and, in some cases, even their lives. Since they are breaking the law, they also risk getting caught and arrested. They risk their freedom. They risk their future. And they do it all for the sake of drugs.

The fact that so many drug users hurt themselves is bad enough. But people who use illegal drugs put everyone else at risk, too. That's another reason why we have laws about some drugs. For instance, each year drug use is the cause of an enormous number of accidents—at home, in the office or workplace, and on the road. Drug users hurt other people in many other ways. Everyone has to pay the costs of drug abuse: the costs of more police officers and prisons, the costs of more hospitals and treatment centers, the costs of time lost at work, and the costs of many promising young lives lost.

But drug users hurt other people most of all because they support the violent criminal activity of the drug network.

Just by using drugs, people become part of that network. They are already committing a crime. But the "straight-line relationship" between drug use and crime often means that drug users go on to commit other crimes—crimes like robbery, burglary, assault, and murder.

Why is there such a strong connection between drug use and crime?

Part of the answer lies in what drugs do to the brain. Drugs change the way the brain works. And they can change the brain so much that it begins to need drugs. This is the start of drug addiction, the constant need or craving for drugs.

Drug addiction means that the brain is "saying" that it needs drugs: it must have drugs. It means that addicts can only think about one thing, only want one thing. It means that addicts feel that they need drugs more than anything. It means that to them drugs *are* more important than work or school, more important than family or friends, more important than life itself.

And it often means that addicts commit crimes to get the money to buy drugs. Research studies clearly show that drug use increases criminal behavior:

- 64 percent of violent crimes involve someone who is using drugs.

- 75 percent of prison inmates have a history of drug use.

- 24 percent of addicts start dealing drugs to support their own drug habits.

One study showed that "addicts committed four times more crime during periods of heavy drug use than in periods when they were drug-free."

Research also indicates that the problem of drug addiction and criminal activity is one that starts with young people:

- More than 83 percent of young people in state prisons have used drugs.

- 40 percent of young people in prison for serious crimes were under the influence of drugs at the time that they committed the offenses for which they were convicted.

- More than 40 percent of young prisoners first used drugs before they were 12 years old. One out of five young prisoners first used drugs before the age of 10.

Many people ask, "Why don't addicts just stop using drugs? Can't they see what drugs are doing to them? Can't they see what drugs are doing to the people around them?"

The fact is that many times they can't. Part of the sickness of drug addiction is that addicts refuse to admit that they have a drug problem. This is called denial. Even when it is obvious to everyone else, addicts can go on fooling themselves. And even when drug addicts do admit that they have a drug problem, it's not easy for them to stop using drugs. Drug addiction is a sickness, and drug addicts need help if they are going to stop using drugs. Addicts can get help, and they can get better. But they need medical attention and counseling if they are to learn how to face life without drugs.

Now let's take a closer look at the reasons why cocaine, heroin, marijuana, and other drugs are considered so dangerous.

COCAINE AND CRACK

"Public enemy number one"—that's what the U.S. Department of Justice calls cocaine.

A recent report from the 93 United States Attorneys notes that "districts all across the country have reported on cocaine's widespread use by people in all walks of life and from all social backgrounds."

And it's not just the big cities that have a cocaine problem. It's western Wisconsin and northern Iowa, where "cocaine is readily available in all communities, to all levels of society." It's the small and mid-sized towns of North Carolina and Kansas, where "the cocaine problem has risen to alarming levels."

This public enemy is a soft, white mixture that might be mistaken for baby powder. But there's no mistaking the effects of cocaine. It is a powerful and sometimes deadly stimulant, a kind of drug that stimulates, or speeds up, the way the body and brain work. Cocaine may be sniffed through the nose or injected directly into the bloodstream with a hypodermic needle. Cocaine users say that the drug produces a strong sense of pleasure, or euphoria.

But it is a dangerous source of pleasure. Cocaine use can cause headaches, vomiting, sore throats, and sinus pain, among many other physical problems. It can lead to sudden death from a heart attack and can cause permanent damage to both the heart and lungs. Cocaine use by pregnant women can seriously hurt their unborn children.

Cocaine also changes the moods and emotions of the people who use it. The repeated use of cocaine can cause people to become confused, nervous, depressed, upset, and overly suspicious of other people. It can cause hallucinations, distortions of normal sights and sounds. And the repeated use of cocaine can quickly lead to drug addiction.

More than 21 million Americans have now used cocaine. In 1990 alone, more than 8 million people used the drug. Some reports estimate that 5,000 new users try cocaine every day.

In recent years, a new form of cocaine called crack has spread across the United States. Crack is a hard, rocklike type of cocaine that is made to be smoked. A highly addictive and dangerous form of cocaine, crack is easy to use and easy to find. Cheap amounts of crack can be bought from street dealers or at crack houses, places where crack is made and sold.

The U.S. government calls crack use "an epidemic of major proportions." In Fort Wayne, Indiana, a city of 182,000 people living in what is sometimes called

America's "heartland," police have identified between 60 and 70 crack houses. From California to Georgia, law enforcement officials report that "the major drug problem today is clearly crack."

HEROIN

They're black, white, and Hispanic. They're male and female. Two out of every three of them are 30 years old or older. One out of every 10 of them is between the ages of 12 and 17.

There are between 500,000 and 750,000 of them.

That's how many Americans are now addicted to heroin. And in recent years federal law enforcement agencies have reported "a rapidly increasing activity in the heroin markets."

Not only is heroin more readily available today, but there are also indications that, in certain regions, heroin use is spreading outside the major cities to the suburbs, mid-sized towns, and even rural areas. Drug investigators have identified such unlikely places as Providence, Rhode Island, and Durham, North Carolina, as new regional heroin distribution centers.

Heroin is the strongest and most addictive of the opiates, a group of drugs made from the juice of the opium poppy. Opiates are also called narcotics. The term "narcotic" means "to make numb" and refers to the fact that such drugs are able to ease pain. In fact, when used under proper medical supervision, morphine and codeine, a much less powerful narcotic, can be very valuable medicines. But there is no medical use for heroin in the United States today.

Although heroin powder may be sniffed through the nose, it is most commonly dissolved in water and then injected into the bloodstream with a hypodermic needle. Heroin produces a strong sense of pleasure, or euphoria, but like the other opiate drugs, heroin also depresses, or slows down, the way the body and brain work. Too strong a dose of heroin, called an overdose, can even shut down the messages that keep the lungs breathing. Each year, thousands of addicts die from heroin overdoses, and hundreds of unborn babies are hurt because pregnant women used the drug.

Heroin users have to face many other problems, too. Many addicts lose interest in food and suffer from malnutrition. Since heroin stops the sensation of pain, addicts often don't know when they have been hurt or need medical treatment. And heroin addicts also run the risk of getting infectious diseases (like hepatitis, tetanus, and AIDS) by sharing used or dirty needles.

In recent years, drug investigators have seen "a dramatic increase in heroin production." In addition, a new and more powerful form of Mexican heroin has made its way onto the American drug scene. Called "black tar," this cheap and very deadly drug has been blamed for a recent rise in overdose deaths.

44

MARIJUANA

Armed patrols. Booby traps. Search and destroy missions. Helicopter surveillance.

Does this sound like American soldiers at war? In a way, it is. But it may not be the way you think. This is a picture of American soldiers at war here in the United States. The battlefields are our national parks and forests. And the enemy is marijuana.

Marijuana is the most widely used illegal drug in the United States:

- More than 65 million people in the United States have used marijuana.

- More than 25 million people have used marijuana in the last year.

- More than 11 million people use marijuana once a month.

- More than 6 million people use marijuana every day.

Marijuana is made from the leaves and flowering tops of the cannabis plant. The cannabis plant contains over 400 chemicals, but the effects of marijuana are largely due to one of these: tetrahydrocannabinol, or THC. The THC in marijuana changes the chemical balance of the brain, causing a light-headed kind of feeling. It also makes it difficult to think clearly, to pay attention, to perform simple tasks, and to remember things. And it can change people's moods, making them unusually nervous or depressed.

Marijuana is usually smoked in cigarettes called joints. But smoking a joint is even more dangerous than smoking a tobacco cigarette. In fact, some recent studies show that smoking one marijuana cigarette may be as harmful as smoking five cigarettes made of tobacco. The many chemicals in marijuana smoke can damage the cells of the brain and nervous system and lead to lung cancer. New studies suggest that there may also be a link between smoking marijuana and heart disease. And because marijuana can destroy the body's disease-fighting white blood cells, people who use it are more likely to get sick than other people.

Marijuana is far less addictive than drugs like cocaine and heroin, and there are people who feel that marijuana is safe enough for adults to use. But the repeated use of marijuana does lead to some long-term changes in the way the brain works. It can make people nervous or anxious. It can make them moody or depressed when they try to stop using marijuana. Long-term use can even cause people to lose interest in everything else but smoking marijuana. This feeling that nothing in life is worth doing is called amotivational syndrome.

Marijuana may be less addictive than cocaine or heroin, but people can easily begin to depend on it as a way of avoiding or escaping the everyday problems and pressures everyone has to face. A recent study of marijuana users shows that they "smoke marijuana to avoid dealing with their difficulties." The same study also reports that when people use marijuana to try to run away from their problems, "it only makes their problems worse."

OTHER DANGEROUS DRUGS

Though cocaine and crack, heroin, and marijuana are the most widely used illegal drugs, they aren't the only ones that form important parts of the illegal drug network in the United States.

• STIMULANTS

Over the past decade, law enforcement officials have seen "an explosive growth" in the use of synthetic, or laboratory-made, stimulants. The most common synthetic stimulant is called methamphetamine, popularly known as "meth," "speed," or "crank." It is either injected into the bloodstream with a hypodermic needle or swallowed as a capsule or tablet. A new form of methamphetamine, one that is called "crystal meth" or "ice," is made to be smoked.

Like other stimulants, methamphetamine speeds up the way the body and brain work. Some users take stimulant drugs to be more alert and energetic, but using stimulants can be very dangerous. Stimulants can cause serious and permanent damage to the body, including stomach ulcers, skin disorders, weight loss, brain damage, and diseases of the lungs, liver, kidneys, and heart. An overdose can cause death from a severe heart attack, the bursting of blood vessels in the brain (a stroke), or the sudden failure of the lungs to keep breathing.

The repeated use of stimulants can also change the moods and emotions of the people who use them, making them very nervous, depressed, or suspicious of other people. And the long-term use of these drugs may lead to severe mental illness.

The use of methamphetamine has spread quickly from the western regions of the United States, especially the southern California area, to cities and towns everywhere. Several areas of the country now report that the use of methamphetamine is as great as the cocaine and crack problem. The U.S. Justice Department has delivered a clear warning on the dangers of this synthetic stimulant: "Methamphetamine may soon become the crack problem of the 1990s."

• HALLUCINOGENS

Another group of synthetic substances that make up a part of the drug network are the hallucinogens. Hallucinogens cause distortions of sights and sounds, and these changes in the way the world appears are called hallucinations. The two most frequently used hallucinogens are LSD, commonly called "acid," and PCP, also known as "angel dust." These drugs can change everyday sights and sounds in strange, confusing, and sometimes frightening ways.

Pure LSD is a white powder. This tasteless and odorless drug is often sold as a tablet or capsule. As a liquid, it can be added to sugar cubes, to thin squares of gelatin called "window panes," or to a special kind of absorbent tissue called "blotter" paper.

Although pure LSD cannot be tasted or smelled, the effects of this drug are very powerful. In fact, LSD is one of the strongest drugs ever made. A speck of LSD no bigger than the period you see at the end of this sentence can cause hallucinations. It can also increase blood pressure, make the heart beat faster, and cause headaches, numbness, nausea, blurred vision, and muscle tremors.

Like LSD, pure PCP is also a white powder, but "on the street" it is sold and used in several forms. It can be injected into the bloodstream with a hypodermic needle, swallowed in tablet or capsule form, or sniffed through the nose. PCP powder can also be sprinkled on marijuana cigarettes and smoked.

Using PCP raises the heart rate and can lead to high blood pressure and heart failure. Using PCP disrupts muscular control and can cause convulsions, a violent and uncontrollable shaking of the muscles. Using PCP can cause lung failure, brain damage, and coma (a deep and prolonged sleep). And what PCP does to the mind is equally bad. It can produce very frightening hallucinations. Some users become violent and angry; others become confused and depressed.

As with many other drugs, the repeated use of hallucinogens can cause long-term changes in mood and personality.

As dangerous as these drugs are, it may surprise you to learn that the use of drugs has not always been against the law. In fact, in some places around the world, drugs like cocaine, marijuana, opiates, and hallucinogens have been used legally for thousands of years. Even in the United States, these drugs were used legally for most of our country's history.

How were these drugs used in the past? What problems did they cause? And why were laws passed to restrict or prohibit them? These are a few of the questions that can only be answered by looking at the history of drugs and crime.

5

Drugs and Crime: A History

There is nothing new about the use of drugs. People have used drugs for thousands of years.

- Opiate drugs were used as medicine more than 6,000 years ago by the people of the Middle East. About 4,000 years ago, the juice of the opium poppy helped calm the crying babies of Egypt. The Greek physician Hippocrates, who is often called the father of modern medicine, also prescribed opiate medicines for his patients. The use of these medicines continued for thousands of years.

- More than 3,000 years ago, the coca plant was part of the everyday life of the Incas of South America. Chewing the coca leaf gave them the energy they needed to farm the rough valleys of the Andes Mountains. Coca was also a part of their religious ceremonies. The Incas believed that if coca leaves were pressed against the mouth of a dead person, "his soul would go to paradise." In fact, the coca plant was so important to these ancient people that they considered it a gift from the gods.

- A medical book from ancient China, written 5,000 years ago, contains what may be the oldest mention of marijuana. From Asia to the Middle East, from Europe to Africa, marijuana was used for centuries as a medicine to treat a variety of sicknesses and to ease or reduce pain. But there were many other uses for marijuana as well. The strong fibers of the cannabis plant were used to make rope and fabrics. Even the seeds of the plant were put to use to make birdseed. And when the leaves of the cannabis plant were pressed, they produced an oil that could be used to help make a quick-drying paint.

- The use of hallucinogens goes back more than 10,000 years. Natural hallucinogenic drugs (like peyote and mescaline) were part of a religious way of life for many ancient people. They considered the hallucinations brought on by the use of these drugs to be "visions" from the gods. These visions were believed to give them special powers: to see what would happen in the future, to talk to their dead ancestors, to explain the meaning of dreams, and to heal the sick and diseased.

When these ancient people used drugs, there were rules about how to use them. Some of these rules were written down. Some of them were not. But whether they were written or unwritten, the rules about drug use had been decided upon by the community. They were part of a code of behavior that the society as a whole thought was acceptable.

Of course, not everybody thought that drug use was acceptable. Throughout the centuries, there have been people who wanted to see that the use of drugs was against the law. In 1378, the leader of one Middle Eastern sheikdom ordered marijuana users to be put in prison. He even ordered that people caught using marijuana should have their teeth pulled out!

About 200 years later, the soldiers of Spain tried to stop the Incas from using the coca leaf. The Spanish soldiers had conquered the native people of the "New World" and made them work as slaves. These conquerors wanted to outlaw coca because they thought that it kept the Incas from becoming Christians. (But the Spanish conquerors changed their minds when they saw that the coca leaf helped their Indian slaves to work harder and longer.)

One of the most dramatic efforts to outlaw drug use occurred in China. The emperor of China wanted to stop the use of opium. Despite strict laws that had been passed in the 1700s to control opium use, there were millions of Chinese people addicted to smoking opium. By the 1830s, more than 2,000 tons of opium were being imported into China each year, largely by British trading groups.

To stop an epidemic of opium addiction that was threatening to destroy Chinese society, the emperor ordered strict punishment, including the death penalty, for drug users and traders. And he passed laws to stop British and other merchants from bringing more opium into China.

But Great Britain went to war with China to protect the profits of its opium trade. China's defeat in the Opium Wars of 1839 and 1856 meant that Great Britain's opium business would continue for many years—and that millions more of the Chinese people would become addicted to opium.

Although there was always opposition to the use of drugs, drug use continued to be a part of daily life for many societies. And one country that permitted the use of cocaine, the opiates, and marijuana was the United States.

MARIJUANA IN AMERICA

In America, the marijuana plant was grown for its fiber from the 1600s to the time of the Civil War. One study reports that marijuana was "a major crop in North America" and played "an important role" in the new and growing American economy.

In the 1800s and early 1900s, marijuana was also used as a medicine. Medical books commonly recommended marijuana as a good treatment for tetanus, cholera, headaches, asthma, depression, and insanity, among other things. Marijuana was also used by women to ease the pains of childbirth.

OPIATES IN AMERICA

The Chinese were not the only ones with an opium problem in the 1800s. America had an opium problem of its own. Actually, the United States had three opium problems:

• Opium Smoking

Thousands of Chinese immigrants came to the American west in the 1850s and 1860s to help build the railroads. They brought much of their culture, or way of life, with them. One of the customs they continued was smoking opium. Some of them opened opium "dens," places where people would come to smoke the drug. It was not long before American men and women, in the words of one report, "were smoking side by side with the Chinese."

• Morphine Addiction

Two nineteenth-century medical discoveries— morphine and the hypodermic needle—made opiate addiction even more likely than it had been before. Morphine (named for Morpheus, the Greek god of sleep and dreams) was 10 times stronger than opium.

And the hypodermic syringe allowed doctors to inject this powerful painkiller directly into the bloodstream. During the Civil War, morphine injections were given to thousands of wounded soldiers, and many of them became addicted to this opiate drug. Morphine addiction was so common among soldiers, in fact, that it became known as "the soldier's disease."

• Other Opiate Medicines

By far the most serious opiate problem in the 1800s was the use of over-the-counter and prescription medicines containing opiate drugs. People took these opiate medicines for such minor aches and pains as headaches and for such common complaints and problems as sleeplessness, nervousness, and diarrhea. Opiate medicines were even given to children to ease teething pain.

It is important to keep in mind that these opiate medicines were legal and very readily available. Doctors prescribed them often, and they could be bought in many places without a prescription: in drugstores, in grocery stores, and even through the mail. Even heroin, the strongest of the opiate drugs, was sold as a cure for coughs and colds. By 1906, there were more than 50,000 opiate medicines easily available.

COCAINE IN AMERICA

In 1859, doctors thought they had found a new "wonder drug." They had discovered a way to extract the active ingredient, cocaine, from the coca leaf. Doctors and scientists began to experiment with cocaine. Many of them, including the famous scientist Sigmund Freud, wrote that cocaine was a cure for everything from fatigue to heartburn, from depression to morphine addiction.

The use of cocaine spread quickly. Like opiates, cocaine was included in many of the over-the-counter medicines and "health" products that flooded the United States in the 1800s. It was also made a part of many other products. New drinks, including a wine and cocaine mixture called Vin Mariani, contained the drug. Such notable Americans as President William McKinley and the inventor Thomas Edison drank Vin Mariani. Metcalf's Coca Wine was one of many such products. Made "From Fresh Coca Leaves," this drink was advertised as "A Pleasant Tonic and Invigorator." In 1886, a new drink contained cocaine. Its name was Coca-Cola. Coca-Cola advertisements said the drink "eased the Tired Brain, soothed the Rattled Nerves, and restored Wasted Energy to both Mind and Body."

For more than two centuries, drugs had been an accepted and legal part of the American way of life. By the late 1880s, more people were using drugs than ever before. Then, within two decades, opium and cocaine would be outlawed. Heroin and marijuana would soon be added to the list of illegal drugs.

What caused this sudden change?

The popularity of drugs like opium and cocaine in the late 1800s made one thing very clear: these drugs were highly addictive. The widespread use of drugs like heroin and cocaine led to a growing public and scientific concern about the dangers of addiction. Reversing his earlier, favorable view of cocaine, Freud reported the terrible effects of cocaine addiction. The newspapers and popular magazines ran hundreds of stories about the horrors of being addicted to drugs. And doctors began to search for more effective and safer medicines.

The problem of addiction was now clear. It was certainly clear to the people who made Coca-Cola. In 1903, the Coca-Cola Company took the cocaine out of its popular drink.

It is hard to know how many Americans suffered from addiction. One estimate says that there were as many as one million people addicted to opium in the United States, while other studies say the figure may be closer to 250,000. Whatever the exact number of addicts, many people thought that drugs presented a major national and international health problem—and that something had to be done to stop the spread of drug addiction.

What most people felt had to be done was to pass laws against the use of drugs. The early 1900s saw the first of hundreds of laws, passed at both the state and national (or federal) level, that were designed to stop or limit the use of drugs. Here are some of the major federal laws and what they said:

- The Pure Food and Drug Act of 1906

This act required that any medicines containing opium or cocaine had to list the drug on their labels. Later additions to the act said that the amount of each drug had to be stated and that medicines containing opium or cocaine also had to meet certain standards of purity.

- The Harrison Narcotic Act of 1914

In 1912, the United States signed an international agreement, known as the Hague Convention, aimed at stopping the international drug trade. To meet its obligations under this drug treaty, the U.S. Congress passed the Harrison Narcotic Act. This act regulated the sale of cocaine and opiates and restricted the use of these drugs to medical purposes. This restriction meant that addicts could no longer obtain drugs from doctors to continue their addiction. It meant that many doctors, in the words of one medical journal, "simply decided to have as little to do as possible with drug addicts or their needs." In 1924, heroin was added to the list of restricted drugs covered by the Harrison Narcotic Act.

- The Marijuana Tax Act of 1937

Like the Harrison Narcotic Act, this act regulated and restricted the use of marijuana. Under this law, marijuana could only be used as medicine, and doctors who prescribed marijuana as medicine (as well as marijuana growers and pharmacists who made and sold marijuana products) had to apply for a special government license. Although the Marijuana Tax Act did not outlaw the medical use of marijuana, it did encourage the state governments to pass tougher anti-marijuana laws. In the years ahead, state after state did just that. The state of Georgia, in fact, made the sale of marijuana to a young person a crime that was punishable by death.

But even with these new laws, America's drug problem only got worse. In fact, some medical and legal authorities argued that these laws actually made the problem of drugs and crime worse. They claimed that the anti-drug laws were forcing drug addicts, as one leading medical journal said, "to the underworld where he can get his drug in violation of the law." In 1915, *American Medicine* reported that drug users had to get opium and cocaine from "depraved criminals." It complained that addicts were "now under the control of the worst elements of society."

Three years later, when a U.S. government panel studied drug use, the problem of drugs and crime had not been eased. More people were using opiates and cocaine than had been using them before the Harrison Narcotic Act was passed. And, even worse, a national network of "dope peddlers" had been established, a network that smuggled large supplies of illegal drugs through seaports and over the Canadian or Mexican border crossings.

The panel's recommendation was a simple one: tougher laws and stricter law enforcement. And in the decades ahead, the individual states passed hundreds of new anti-drug laws. Between 1914 and 1970, the U.S. Congress also passed more than 50 additions to the Harrison Narcotic Act.

In 1970, the U.S. Congress passed the Drug Abuse Prevention and Control Act. This new act created five categories, or "schedules," of different drugs depending on how dangerous they were. It also made the anti-drug penalties tougher than ever before. In 1981, the United States declared a war on drugs, and the U.S. Congress passed new laws to give the government the legal "weapons" it needed to fight this war. The new federal anti-drug laws were toughened by more laws: the Comprehensive Crime Control Act of 1984, the Anti-Drug Abuse Act of 1986, and the Anti-Drug Abuse Act of 1988.

But new laws and tougher penalties alone were not enough to stop the drug trade. In fact, during the 1970s and 1980s, as new and tougher anti-drug laws were being passed, the use of drugs by Americans soared. By 1986, Americans were using 60 percent of the world's supply of illegal drugs. U.S. drug sales were running at more than $100 billion a year. That's more money than American farmers make each year from all the crops they sell. That's more money than General Motors, the country's biggest business, makes in a year.

In recent years, there have been some signs that anti-drug laws are working. A recent survey by the National Institute on Drug Abuse indicates that the number of people now using drugs is decreasing. But it will take more than tough laws to stop the drug trade. It will take money to pay for the police and the military operations, for the different kinds of medical treatment, and for new ways to teach people about the danger of illegal drugs.

It will take more than money. It will take more than prisons and treatment centers and educational programs. The problem is people. And the answer is people—the people who understand the "straight-line relationship" between drug use and crime and care enough to do something about it. It will take people who care enough to say "No" to drugs.

6

Alcohol: The Deadliest Drug

What drug is involved in more crimes than any other?

a. cocaine	d. marijuana
b. heroin	e. PCP
c. LSD	f. amphetamines

Which answer did you pick? If you picked any of these answers, then you were wrong.

The answer is alcohol.

This may not seem like a fair test, but there's a good reason for tricking you. Most people don't think of alcohol as a drug. But it is. In fact, it is one of the most dangerous and costly drugs of all.

- Each year, 100,000 people die from sicknesses due to alcohol.

- Each year, 500,000 people enter alcohol treatment programs.

- About one out of every four families has a member with a drinking problem.

- Each year, problems caused by alcohol cost the U.S. economy over $100 billion.

Alcohol is a kind of drug called a depressant. This means that alcohol depresses, or slows down, the messages that travel to and from the brain. It slows down the messages that control our senses, making it hard for people to see and hear clearly. Alcohol makes it hard for people to walk a straight line and even to stand up because it disrupts the messages that control body movement. Alcohol makes it hard for people to pay attention and to remember things, too, because it slows down the messages that control our thoughts. And alcohol also disrupts the messages that control our emotions, making people suddenly happy or sad, suddenly upset, angry, or depressed.

Alcohol can change the way the brain works in another important way. It is a very addictive drug. Dr. Charles Schuster, the director of the National Institute on Drug Abuse, says that the number of people in the United States with an alcohol problem is about 17 million. That's six times higher than the number of people who are addicted to cocaine and crack. Worse, the evidence indicates that the number of alcoholics is now increasing.

"There's no question about it," Dr. Schuster adds, "alcohol remains the number-one drug problem in the United States."

Because of its effects on the brain, alcohol is a leading cause of accidents. According to the National Council on Alcoholism, alcohol is a "contributing factor" in more than 15,000 deaths and 6 million injuries due to accidents each year. One out of four serious accidents involves alcohol. Nearly seven out of every 10 drowning deaths involve alcohol.

And because of its effects on the brain, alcohol is a leading cause of crime. One survey estimates that more than 40 percent of all arrests made by the police are directly related to alcohol. Many other arrests are for crimes indirectly related to the use of alcohol, such as disorderly conduct.

Here is what one leading researcher has to say about the "straight-line relationship" between alcohol and violent crime:

> "Of all the popular drugs, alcohol is most consistently and strongly linked with crime, especially such crimes as homicide, assault, rape, and child beating. Alcohol turns up again and again as a factor in these crimes. . . . In short, alcohol, more than any other single drug, plays a major role in crime, especially those types of crime resulting in physical injury."

The point is clear: alcohol often leads to violent crime. It may be a murder on the streets. One study shows that as many as 50 percent of prison inmates arrested for crimes like murder and assault had been drinking when they committed violent acts. Or it may be an assault in the home. The National Council on Alcoholism notes that 63 percent of women who are violently abused by their husbands report "that their husbands were drinking when they were violent."

And one violent crime involving alcohol use is frequently forgotten, although it is committed more often than any other crime in the United States. It is drinking and driving. Almost 2 million people every year are arrested for drunk driving. That's more than three times the number of people arrested for all other violent crimes combined!

Picture a clock ticking away. Every 60 seconds the second hand sweeps around the face of the clock. Another minute has passed.

There's a lot that can happen in a minute. Every 60 seconds someone is seriously injured in a drunk driving crash. Drunk driving crashes injure more than 650,000 people each year.

Every 60 minutes the minute hand makes its way around the clock. Another hour has passed.

A lot can happen in an hour. Every hour three people are killed in drunk driving crashes. That's an average of one death every 20 minutes. Drunk driving crashes kill nearly 24,000 people each year.

Every 24 hours another day has passed. And every day 10 teenagers die in drunk driving crashes—more than 3,600 teenagers each year. Drinking and driving is the number-one killer of teenagers.

It's against the law for people to drink too much and drive. That's just one of many laws passed by the states to restrict the sale and use of alcoholic products. But not too long ago, from 1920 to 1933, alcohol was completely outlawed by an amendment to the Constitution of the United States. The Eighteenth Amendment to the U.S. Constitution started the period in American history known as Prohibition.

It may surprise you to learn that there was a time when alcohol was outlawed. It may also surprise you to learn that, in the 1700s and 1800s, Americans were drinking so much alcohol that our country was called "a nation of drunkards."

Many people thought that Americans were drinking *too* much. They wanted to temper, or limit, the use of alcohol, and they formed the American temperance movement. There were other people who thought that Americans shouldn't be using any alcoholic products. They wanted to prohibit, or stop, the sale and use of alcohol. These people were called prohibitionists, and they formed several powerful political parties to stop America's drinking habits. In the early 1900s, many states passed new prohibition laws. And on January 16, 1920, the Eighteenth Amendment to the U.S. Constitution made "the manufacture, sale, or transportation of intoxicating liquors" illegal everywhere in the United States.

The Eighteenth Amendment outlawed alcoholic products, but that didn't stop people from drinking them. One way or another, many people continued their drinking habits. Illegal alcoholic products, called "bootleg" liquor, were made in the United States or smuggled across the Mexican and Canadian borders. Bootleg liquor found its way into many homes and into private clubs called "speakeasies." It even found its way into the White House.

Illegal liquor also found its way into the hands of criminal gangs. During the 1920s, ruthless gangsters fought—and often killed—one another to gain control of the manufacture and sale of alcoholic products.

To mobsters like Al Capone, selling alcohol was "just a business." But, like the modern cocaine trade, it was a ruthless and bloody business. It was a business that took the lives of many police officers, federal agents, and innocent bystanders.

Some people argue that Prohibition was actually a public health success. They point out that the number of alcohol-related illnesses decreased during this period. But for many people at the time, the Prohibition experiment seemed to be a failure. It didn't seem to prevent people from using alcohol, and it seemed to bring violence and bloodshed to the streets of our cities. By the early 1930s, most people wanted to see the law changed. Once again, it took an amendment to the Constitution of the United States. On December 5, 1933, the national drinking law was changed. This time, the Twenty-First Amendment ended the 13-year Prohibition period.

Once again, it was up to the states to make their own laws about alcoholic products, and in the years ahead, the states did pass different laws about who could make alcoholic products, where and when they could be sold, and who could drink them. Today, the laws about drinking alcohol are tougher than at any time since Prohibition ended. The legal drinking age (the age at which people may legally use alcohol) is now the same in every state. You must be 21 years old to buy or use alcohol anywhere in the United States. And hundreds of communities have passed strict laws against drinking and driving.

But tough laws alone are not the answer to the problem of alcohol and crime. As with other drugs, the problem is people. The problem is people who don't think that alcohol can be a dangerous drug. The problem is people who don't think about what alcohol does to the body and brain. The problem is people who don't think before they drink and drive.

As with other drugs, the answer to the problem of alcohol and crime is people. It's people who are smart enough to know that just because a drug is legal for adults, that doesn't mean it is always safe to use. It's people who are strong enough not to give in to peer pressure to drink alcohol. And it's people like you—young people—who are determined enough to make the future a happy, healthy, and safe one.

7

The War on Drugs:
An Interview with William Alden

The drug trade is a worldwide business. Stopping that trade is the job of thousands of men and women. They work for local and state police departments. They work for national law enforcement agencies, like the Federal Bureau of Investigation, the Department of Justice, the U.S. Customs Service, and many others. They work in the fields of health, education, and counseling. They are part of an anti-drug effort that may cost as much as $12 billion each year. It's their job to disrupt and destroy the drug network.

One of these drug fighters is William F. Alden. William Alden works for the Drug Enforcement Administration (DEA). He is the Chief of Congressional and Public Affairs and the Director of the Demand Reduction Programs. As Alden knows, stopping the drug trade means reducing two things: the supply of drugs and the demand for them. Stopping the drug trade means attacking every part of the drug network. It means putting the drug business out of business.

One way to reduce the drug supply is to destroy the network's source of raw materials, the crops from which drugs come, and the refineries where drugs are processed. Destroying the drug plants is called crop eradication. Thousands of acres of drug crops, both in the United States and abroad, are destroyed each year. The United States also pays many farmers to grow other crops, helping them to make a decent living without being part of the drug network. To attack the drug refineries, Latin American and U.S. military forces destroy hundreds of jungle labs each year.

But it is not enough. Each year the production of illegal drugs increases.

Another way to reduce the supply of drugs is to disrupt drug shipment routes. Stopping the flow of drug smuggling is called drug interdiction. Officials of the U.S. Customs Service check tens of thousands of people, pieces of luggage, and vehicles entering the United States every day. Customs agents patrol our national borders day and night, searching for suspicious ships and planes.

But it is not enough. It is estimated that U.S. drug interdiction efforts catch no more than 10 percent of the drugs shipped to the United States. As the former Customs Commissioner, William von Raab, says, "It's just like building a sandcastle. You build a good wall here, the sea starts coming in somewhere else."

Even if the supply of foreign drugs could be stopped, that would not solve America's drug problem. Carlton Turner, a former White House drug policy adviser, is one of many drug fighters who says that America's drug problem is an *American* problem:

> *"You can put up wall-to-wall policemen, wall-to-wall Coast Guard ships, wall-to-wall aircraft. You can do away with every cannabis plant in the world, every coca bush, every opium poppy, and you'd still have a drug problem in this country."*

State and local law enforcement officials try to reduce the supply of drugs by destroying the drug network's distribution system. They arrest thousands of dealers and users each year. They raid crack houses and set up "sting" operations to catch drug buyers. These anti-drug efforts cost over $5 billion each year.

But it is not enough. "Law enforcement can only hold the line," says Charles Blau, a former top Justice Department assistant. "It can keep the drug situation from getting much worse. But we'll never solve the problem with law enforcement alone."

There has to be something more. There has to be a reduction in the demand for drugs. In the following interview, William Alden says that the drug problem is a problem of attitude. The "something more" that will finally win the war on drugs, Alden says, is a change in attitude—a change that will send out the message that America is determined to be drug-free.

What is the most important part of the war on drugs?

The most important part is attitude. It's developing an anti-drug attitude. And it's not just caring about *your* actions. It's caring enough about other people to send them an anti-drug message.

How does this anti-drug message get sent?

Role modeling is crucial. But you shouldn't have to look past the kitchen table for a role model. The war on drugs begins right there—at the kitchen table. It begins right there at home. It begins in the family. It works through your neighbors and your community. It works through the schools and the churches.

How does the anti-drug message work?

It begins with taking responsibility for your actions—and for each other. The reason we have a drug problem is that we developed an attitude that says, "Well, I can do to myself what I want, and it's not going to hurt anyone else." Now we have found out that's just not true.

Do other countries have such a big drug problem?

The drug problem is not just an American problem. An interesting thing is beginning to take place around the world: the rest of the world is beginning to realize that America has suffered dramatically from the drug epidemic. Suffered from it, but learned from it, too. And other countries around the world are looking at us and saying, "If this is what can happen to the greatest democracy in the world, what would drugs do to our country?"

Now they're looking at America for direction because they see that we have begun, at last, to change attitudes. The world position now is that America is beginning to turn things around. Other countries are saying, "We must try to get more assistance from the United States. If nothing else, we need to learn from the Americans not to repeat any of the mistakes that they made."

What mistakes did we make?

The mistake we made was primarily in developing a drug-tolerant attitude. We needed to develop an anti-drug attitude. But we didn't do it.

We didn't do it at the national level. We didn't do it at the family level. If anything, we sent young people mixed messages about drugs—or no message at all. We fooled ourselves as a society. We sent a message that said, "If I decide to use drugs, there are no consequences." The message of the war on drugs is that there are consequences.

But are people who use drugs really hurting other people?

Yes. When anyone uses drugs, everyone pays the price. There is no such thing as "casual" drug use. That's very misleading. Drug users hurt their fellow employees and family members. They hurt strangers on the road. Drugs users are responsible for the lives that are lost—the lives of their friends hurt by drugs, the lives of law enforcement officials that are lost in Colombia, in Mexico, and in America. There are costs to using drugs that affect all of us. So-called "casual" drug users are part of the problem. And they were ignored for a long time. That's how we developed this drug-tolerant attitude.

But are we really in a war on drugs?

Yes. The war on drugs is a reaction to what drugs have done—and are doing—to our society. They have brought death and destruction just as a military war would have done.

That's why it takes nothing short of an all-out war to overcome the drug problem.

Drug use costs America. Just think for a moment about the economic costs. What are the consequences? What does that mean for every one of us?

And there is so much suffering. There are babies who are born addicted to crack because their mothers are crack addicts. Think about the harm and suffering that they are born with when they enter this world. Think about the social impact of that fact. Will these children ever be healthy and happy? Will they ever be productive citizens? How do you put a price tag on that suffering?

Who is the enemy in this war on drugs?

Everyone who is part of the drug culture is the enemy. The enemy are the drug groups who control the illegal drug trade, the producers who make illegal drugs, the smugglers who bring illegal drugs into the country, the dealers who sell the drugs on the street, and the people who buy and use drugs.

How do we defeat this enemy?

One way to get rid of the drug problem is to get rid of, or eradicate, illegal drugs. Stop the drug problem at the source. One way to get rid of the problem is to get rid of the plant sources of the illegal drugs. Remove the plant sources. Pull the drug crops right out of the ground. Destroy them. If there are no illegal drug crops available for processing, then there are no illegal drugs available to use.

But that can't always be successful. So there are different ways. Investigate the path of the drug trade and stop drug shipments. That's one part, but only one part. If we had the ability as a nation to put up a wall to keep out all the illegal drugs that are produced in countries around the world, well, we would still have a serious drug problem.

We have to arrest those people who profit from the drug trade. Send them to jail, and take away the money they make from drugs. Make people see the consequences of drug use. Make them feel the consequences of drug use.

Education is a part of the war on drugs: reinforcing the anti-drug message, teaching people to resist peer pressure. Our kids are being asked to make the most important decision of their lives. And it's a decision that's made harder by peer pressure, because one of the reasons kids use drugs is that other kids use drugs. Peer pressure begins at an early age and continues for the rest of our lives.

Testing and treatment—these are all parts of the war on drugs.

It takes all these parts. It all adds up. And it all begins to change attitudes.

Who's winning the drug war?

We are. We're beginning to see changes. We're beginning to see success. The consequences of using drugs are higher today. Things have changed. If you get caught, then you'll spend time in jail. You'll lose the money you made. The stakes are higher today. It's becoming more difficult to do business in drugs in the United States.

Some people say our society cannot afford this war. How do you respond to that?

The cost of the drug war is not nearly as great as the cost of continuing to accept drug use.

Can this war be won?

Our goal is a drug-free America. Any less than that would not be true to our nature. I feel good when I drive by a school and see the signs that say, "Drug-Free School Zone." That's important. The children are our natural resources. They are the most important resource we have. And we're going to make a statement about them. If this had been done 10 years ago, we wouldn't have this kind of drug problem today. That's the kind of message we're going to send.

William Alden is one of the thousands of people who work for the Drug Enforcement Administration. The DEA is only one of many national, state, and local law enforcement agencies fighting to stop the illegal drug trade. And, as William Alden points out, law enforcement is only one part of our national anti-drug effort, an anti-drug campaign that includes programs in education and treatment. There are thousands of "soldiers" in the war on drugs.

But the war on drugs won't be won by these men and women alone. The change in attitudes that will win the war on drugs is not just the job of the police or the job of federal drug agents. It's not just the job of teachers, counselors, and health workers.

The drug problem is everyone's problem.

And the job of fighting drugs is everyone's job.

8

The Drug-Free Network

Now you know about the "straight-line relationship" between drugs and crime. Now you know how all the pieces of the drug puzzle fit together.

You know that drugs are part of a vast network of criminal activity. It is a network that stretches from the poppy fields of Southeast Asia to the streets of New York City, from the mountains of the Colombian countryside to the homes of small-town America. And now you've seen some of the true pictures of the drug network at work.

You know that drugs are dangerous and that the people who deal drugs are dangerous, too. You know that drug dealers don't care who gets hurt by drugs. You know that they don't care who gets hurt by drug-related violence. It's just part of doing business.

You've seen that the network of drugs and crime hurts everyone, whether they use drugs or not. The drug trade costs money that could be spent on schools and parks. It means that we need more police officers to enforce the law. It means that we need more hospital workers to treat the victims of drug-related crimes.

But the drug network can be broken. There are many people working to build a drug-free America. Some people are working to pass laws that will make it harder for drug dealers to do business. Other people are working to disrupt the drug network by eradicating drugs at the source or stopping the shipment of illegal drugs. They are part of the drug-free network.

But it will take more than laws and police and military operations to bring an end to the drug network. As William Alden says, it will take a change in attitude. It will take a drug-free network of families and neighborhoods—a network of people both young and old, a network of people who want healthy lives and safe communities. It will take a network of people who understand the relationship between drugs and crime and care enough to say "No" to drugs.

It may be difficult to say where the drug network begins, but it's not difficult to say where the *drug-free* network begins. It begins with you.

Glossary

addiction the constant need or craving for a drug

alcohol a depressant drug found in beer, wine, and liquor

cartel a combination of groups who work together to increase business

cocaine a stimulant drug made from the coca plant

crack a form of cocaine made to be smoked

crack house a place where crack is made and sold

dealer a person who sells illegal drugs; a pusher

depressant a drug that slows down the way the brain works

distribution the system by which illegal drugs reach the user

eradication destroying the plant sources of illegal drugs

hallucinogen a drug that causes distorted sensory perceptions

heroin one of several opiate drugs

interdiction stopping the flow of drug smuggling

marijuana a drug made from the cannabis, or hemp, plant

narcotic another word for an opiate drug

opiate a drug made from the opium poppy

processing the way drug crops are prepared for use

Prohibition the movement to make alcohol illegal

raw material the plant source from which drugs come

refinery a place where drug crops are processed and prepared for shipment

shipment the movement of illegal drugs from source to user

smuggling bringing drugs into a country illegally

source a plant or place from which drugs come

stimulant a drug that speeds up the way the brain works

Index